The Sandwich Way

ISBN 979-8-88685-908-9 (paperback)
ISBN 979-8-88685-909-6 (digital)

Christian Faith Publishing
832 Park Avenue
Meadville, PA 16335
www.christianfaithpublishing.com

Printed in the United States of America

The Sandwich Way

First Day of School

Jalaila Hardy

Hi! I'm PB, and today is my first day of school!

I get dressed...

I brush my teeth and wash my face...

I even eat breakfast...

Just like the PB&J Sandwich family!

Hi! I'm Geli, and today is
my first day of school!

I get dressed...

I brush my teeth and wash my face...

I even eat breakfast...

Just like the Jelly Sandwich family!

Hi! I'm Nutelia, and today
is my first day of school!

I get dressed...

I brush my teeth and wash my face...

I even eat breakfast...

Just like the Nutella Sandwich family!

Today was our first day of school, and
we did great! Just like sandwiches!

16

We aren't that different after all!